Stage design

PN
2081
S8
R63

Stage design
Kenneth Rowell

111114

Studio Vista : London
Reinhold Book Corporation : New York

A Studio Vista/Reinhold Art Paperback
Edited by John Lewis
© Kenneth Rowell 1968
Published in London by Studio Vista Ltd
Blue Star House, Highgate Hill, London N19
and in New York by Reinhold Book Corporation
a subsidiary of Chapman-Reinhold, Inc.
430 Park Avenue, New York, NY 10022
Library of Congress Catalog Card Number 67–30535
Distributed in Canada by General Publishing Co. Ltd
30 Lesmill Road, Don Mills, Ontario
Set in 9/12 Univers Medium (Monotype Series 689)
Printed in the Netherlands
by NV Drukkerij Koch en Knuttel, Gouda
SBN 289 27758 2 (paperback)
      289 37011 6 (cased)

CONTENTS

Lila de Nobili: Setting for *Love for Love* (Congreve)
The National Theatre Company at the Old Vic,
London, 1966.
Photo: Dominic

John Bury: Setting for *The Homecoming* (Pinter)
Royal Shakespeare Company, London, 1965.
Photo: Reg Wilson

Introduction

Stage design is now recognized as an established and integral part of theatrical production,
so the contemporary stage designer is free to
extend the vocabulary of stage language —
ensuring more vital and meaningful interpretation of dramatic works of the past and present.
New dramatic forms which use subtle mutations
of acting, singing, dancing and mime require a
visual equivalent, and the achievement of this
is a constant challenge to the designer.
If we accept the premise of the inter-relation
of the arts, we see that a designer should be
aware of the entire aesthetic climate of his own
time. A designer who is ignorant of the painting,
sculpture and graphic art being created about
him may only be capable of making a pastiche

of a period (although even that will not be interpreted in terms that belong to his own time),
and plays, operas and ballets from the classical
repertoire need to be re-interpreted according
to the taste and fashions of the time. Else, why
bother to have a work re-designed? The
Victorians were served up with productions of
Shakespeare which interpreted the plays in a
manner and style which seem ludicrous to us —
but which to them were unquestionably illuminating and valid. In matters of scenic and
costume design style and taste prove often to
be ephemeral, and public and critical taste
change rapidly in a medium where novelty is
often mistaken for genuine originality.
The notorious fickleness on the part of critics,

producers and audiences towards designers makes it a medium in which (except for the secure few) it is often difficult to develop, through lack of sufficient opportunities to work constantly in the theatre.

But good stage-designers (like actors) are tenacious, and seize opportunities when they are offered; and if the designers most likely to be permanently employed are those pre-occupied with unimaginative, romantic traditions, the comparatively small body of really creative designers continues to carve a path through the morass of conventional and often bad design.

When the curtain goes up on a production the audience should be able to grasp instantly the style-atmosphere of what is being presented. When this is made to happen the spectator will be sympathetically orientated to the world that is being created before him.

Jointly, producer and designer are responsible for the total stage entity (lighting being considered both as part of design and as part of the producer's dramatic needs).

The unity of vision between scenic elements and the rest of the theatrical components (including the music) will depend on the degree of empathy between the collaborators. Besides finding a way in which to complement scenically the spirit of the production, a designer should be able to provide the director with all the practical requirements necessary for him to manoeuvre his actors in a way convincing to them and to the audience. A work is capable of an infinite number of interpretations, as we can see by comparing the extraordinary variety of readings it may be given; no one conception will endure for more than a brief span as the definitive one. A play, opera or ballet which survives to become part of the classical repertory will, over the years, be sub-jected to periodic re-interpretation. The re-assessment of a work may derive as much from the originality of the designer's vision as from a new understanding of the dramatic content. As any designer who has enjoyed the experience realises, there is nothing so stimulating as the spontaneous reciprocation of ideas that occurs in a really spirited and constructive collaboration, and the director who regards his designer as an equal in the creative process and who is prepared to be stimulated by the designs, is more likely to succeed in achieving a theatrical homogeneity in the final work.

It is difficult to catalogue satisfactorily the more obvious trends in modern stage design, for the truth is that, while there is a wide stylistic range, comparatively little has emerged which is not derived from previous scenic forms.

The exceptions are: (a) the current pre-occupation with materials recently invented and (b) a new awareness of the potential of stage machinery (built to a designer's requirements with the technical assistance of an imaginative consultant engineer) as a means of creating a more mobile type of scenery. Other important trends are discussed fully in Chapter III.

When people refer to something outside the theatre as 'too theatrical', they mean in all probability that it is flamboyant, colourful or even vulgar. Unfortunately much that has been seen in the theatre in recent years errs on the other side. It is not sufficiently theatrical. The Wicked Fairy Good-Taste, lurking in the wings, has touched the work with her pernicious wand! We have all seen productions in which Good Taste has almost eviscerated a masterpiece as if its theatrical guts were unsuitable for public view.

The theatre, which can be an arena for great purity of expression, should also be a place where we can satisfy an atavistic need for ritual and visual splendour; and many works written for the theatre have this in mind: the senses, through the eye, delight in being ravished — witness the recent great success in England and America of such 'Director's Plays' as *The Royal Hunt of The Sun* and the *Marat/Sade*.

The spectacle that attends much opera production is at least part of the attraction for the vast audiences which are drawn to this form of theatre. Further evidence of this can be found in the large-scale musical and the revival of interest in the three-act ballet.

Of course, it is true that some of the most original and important theatre of our time is the antithesis of the visually splendid and lavish; but it is perhaps this very *range* of theatre forms that guarantees the theatre its future — and creates the need for a wide spectrum of designing styles.

A subject as diverse as modern stage design (in terms of world theatre) clearly cannot be considered comprehensively in the present work. The most the writer can do is to give a brief historical outline of stage design in this century and to survey the contemporary scene. In a period so rich in achievement it is impossible to mention more than the key figures — but even here an arbitrary choice must be made and, inevitably, some important designers and producers will be absent from these pages. The standard of design and actual theatre conditions vary considerably from one country to another, but many problems are common to all theatre staging and can be discussed in general terms.

In an age of easy inter-communication the theatre of one particular country need no longer be isolated from current world trends.

Festivals, literary studies and the increased possibility for travel lead to a greater knowledge of the work being done outside one's own country, and for this reason there is much useful cross-fertilising of ideas, while a play which has aroused interest in one country will quickly find translators in others.

Furthermore, directors and designers are invited to work in foreign countries (although there is scope for an exchange of creative talent on a much greater scale), and to work outside a known milieu and to be confronted with alien techniques can be a stimulating and rewarding experience.

If this book is aimed more at the budding student/designer than the established and experienced theatre artist, it is hoped the layman may also be helped to a greater understanding of the place the designer occupies in the modern theatre, and be made more aware of the designer's aims so that he can appreciate — rather more than he would have done otherwise — the designer's rôle in making the play come alive.

It is not intended to deal with the techniques of scene-building, scene-painting or costume-making. Many excellent technical books dealing specifically with the subjects are available and a short bibliography is given on page 96. A glossary of technical terms has been included and is to be found on page 92.

Sketch by Hawes Craven for a scene in a Henry Irving
production at the Lyceum Theatre, London, in 1892.
An example of the form of elaborate Naturalism —
with stress on architectural detail and false perspectives
— characteristic of stage settings at the end of the 19th
Century. It was precisely this kind of Old Master ren-
dering of a scene which such early innovators as Craig
and Appia sought to abolish.

Internationally, the prevailing style in stage design towards the end of the 19th Century was a reflection of much that was reactionary in art and decoration. In stage settings an ornate Naturalism, by turns faded or garish, had been created more by scene-painters than by professional stage-designers or artists.

A total lack of co-ordination existed between setting and costumes, and any careful planning or close collaboration by all those involved in a production was virtually unknown. In these haphazard conditions the leading actors and actresses invariably had their own wardrobes and wore what they pleased, without regard for the ensemble. Not that incongruities of this kind are altogether absent today, especially on the operatic stage: there is a story of a celebrated opera singer appearing, a few years ago, as Susanna in *The Marriage of Figaro* at Covent Garden carrying a handbag with the initial S picked out in diamonds.

The homogeneity of style which had been seen in the magnificent court entertainments, masques and theatre productions of the 17th and 18th Centuries and even in the Romantic theatre of the early 19th Century, was soon to be reinstated as a basic principle of stage design. Gradually, towards the end of the 19th Century, Naturalistic scenery began to replace the charmingly illusionistic stage effects of the Romantic epoch. By 1875 the Duke of Saxe-Meiningen, with his autocratic control of all the elements in the productions (in his State Theatre and later with his troupe which travelled to other parts of Europe including Berlin and Brussels), was achieving a unity of vision lacking in most theatres.

In 1887, in haphazard, almost amateur conditions, the Théâtre Libre was formed — principally through the energies and determination of André Antoine. This employee of the Paris Gas Company was fervently interested in the theatre and was himself actor, producer and responsible for the pieces of 'real', as opposed to property, furnishings borrowed to provide a 'set' for the initial productions. Dubbed Naturalistic by the critics from the outset, much to the chagrin and disgust of Antoine himself who loathed the tag, his style of acting and staging represented a break with prevailing conventions. However crudely at first, the productions — given in an obscure dramatic club in Montmartre, the Cercle Gaulois — proved to be a turning point in theatre history; and Antoine, with the blessing of the arch-Naturalist Émile Zola, became the figurehead in Western Europe of a Naturalist style that was seen to be an irrevocable break with the traditions of the Romantic Theatre.

One of the most powerful manifestations of Naturalism was — and remains today — the Moscow Art Theatre, founded by Konstantin Stanislavsky and Vladimir Nemirovitch-Danchenko. Stanislavsky, one of the most important figures in modern theatre history, has written with great perception on the manner in which director, actor and designer may arrive at the interpretive truth through a deep understanding of the work itself and obsessive attention to every detail of the production.

As we shall see, what was considered most authentic and true for artists working in the Naturalistic style proved unacceptable to the Symbolist designers who were to seek their own synthesis of the elements they found relevant.

The Naturalists believed in the exact reproduction of a known scene or place, using as nearly as possible the *actual* materials and objects belonging to that environment and matching it with a 'natural' style of acting and direction.

It is a paradox that modern stage design has its roots largely in the Russian theatre which has itself rejected the advances made by Russian innovators. As early as 1895 a group of Russian painters, including Serov, Korovin, Vrubel, Maliutin and the brothers Vasnetzov, sought a new, simplified approach to stage design and foresaw a theatre in which there would be a consistent harmony between all the elements involved in the production.

By 1890 Mamontov, a wealthy patron of the arts in Moscow, had conceived the idea of inviting easel-painters to design settings and costumes for his productions of opera, but it was Sergei Diaghilev who, after first presenting exhibitions of Russian art and later in 1908 a season of Russian Opera in Paris, brought his Ballets Russes to Western Europe and changed the course of stage design and production with legendary effect.

Working on a similar premise, but arriving at vastly different stylistic results, a young English actor, Edward Gordon Craig, was making his first experiments in a revolutionary style that aimed at radically simplifying stage design and creating an aesthetically satisfying entity. Craig (who had been an actor in Henry Irving's company and must himself, therefore, have appeared in some of Irving's characteristically opulent productions) was a visionary who saw that the time had come for the stage to be swept clear of perspective-fixated back-drops and Naturalistic scenery with its decorative irrelevancies. Adolphe Appia, a Swiss theatre artist, was another of the innovators of this time who began to prove that it was possible to distil in scenic terms the essence of the theme and mood of the work being presented. In retrospect the new theory seems remarkably simple and obvious: to provide a stage entity conceived as an artistic whole and achieved through form, design, colour and light.

Craig and Appia were among the first to see, in the semipermanent set, or the manipulation in varying juxtaposition of consistent scenic elements, the solution to the problem of staging plays written in short scenes (i.e. the Elizabethan Canon) and assuring dramatic flow, unbroken by long, distracting scene-changes. It was the concept of a setting composed of sculptural and architectural forms which, by being interchangeable and subject to infinite changes of mood by the variable use of lighting, has proved to be the genesis of a vast body of staging in this century.

Diaghilev's Russian Ballet

The first ballets given by the Diaghilev company in Paris were all designed by Russian painters, and were a revelation. Treating the area within the proscenium arch as a vast canvas they brought on to the stage their imagery and painterliness, producing décors of great beauty. Diaghilev had established the fact that art and the theatre are far from incompatible (a fact too often now denied).

Among Diaghilev's early collaborators were Michel Larionov and Natalia Goncharova, whose designs glowed with Russian imagery and iconography, and Alexander Benois, who exerted a great influence on Diaghilev's taste at this time and whose work was more classically motivated. The brilliantly exotic designs

Natalia Goncharova: Act Drop for *Sorochinsky Fair*
(Mussorgsky) Théâtre des Champs-Elysées, Paris, 1926

Russian folklore seen through the eyes of a theatre
artist influenced by the fractured forms of Cubism.

Léon Bakst: Costume design for *La Légende de Joseph* Théâtre de l'Opera, Paris, 1914.
Photo: Victoria and Albert Museum, London

of Léon Bakst, which were to prove such a liberating factor in the use of daring new colour harmonies and pattern-making, were to influence taste far beyond the realms of the theatre, and both his vivid colour and his imagery can be seen translated into fashions and furnishings of the period. Other Russian artists used by Diaghilev in this period were Korovin, Golovine, Roerich, Soudeikine and Dobujinsky. The Diaghilev Company, although based spiritually in Paris, after 1914 became a wanderer over the face of Europe. By 1917, following his successes with Russian artists, Diaghilev began to draw on the most avant-garde easel-painters of the School of Paris.

Until his death in 1929 this astonishing man continued to cause ballets to be created according to his by now recognisable formula. Selecting, with uncanny flair and judgement, choreographer, composer and painter-as-designer to collaborate on a project, he established an ultra-sophisticated kind of theatre enjoyed by a coterie audience. The irony is that Diaghilev, who in his productions originally conceived as the ideal, the perfect balance of dance, music and painting as a collective whole, came eventually to allow the pictorial element too often to dominate his productions, and he was obliged towards the end to satisfy a demand for ever-increasing novelty.

But before this happened Diaghilev gave the world many masterpieces, and the recent revival in England by one of his most original and important choreographers, Bronislava Nijinska, of two ballets commissioned by him — *Les Biches* and *Les Noces* — showed two superbly designed ballets in which the ideal pictorial equivalent to the choreography and music was found. Both works demonstrate the soundness of Diaghilev's original aims.

16

Edward Gordon Craig

Edward Gordon Craig: Figures for the Irish Stage
Photo: Collection Edward Craig

What Diaghilev was doing with the Ballets Russes to reform stage design, Gordon Craig had some years before started to do for the drama in England, and, as his ideas took fire, in Western Europe. As early as 1897 he was aware of the revolution that needed to take place in theatre production and design. With very little training in art, but intense hard work and a profound belief in his vision, he became, in his handling of scenic masses, light and colour, an amazing draughtsman of the theatre. Giving up his job as a successful actor, he spent three years consolidating his theories and acquiring a technique in drawing and making woodcuts. (It is in the latter unlikely medium that many of his later designs were made.)

1900 marks the beginning of his designs actually being realised in the theatre. These were seen only in small theatres for a few performances, and were made possible only through great determination and the enthusiasm and encouragement of a few friends. Writing about Craig's first designs for his mother, Ellen Terry, Count Kessler, one of Craig's most earnest supporters, says: 'They astounded London by their almost fanatical simplification and their turning away from realism'.*

His ideas took immediate root in a country already seeking a new symbolism and purity of form in stage presentation. He had published a book, *The Art of the Theatre*, and exhibited his designs in Germany and Switzerland; Max Reinhardt — whose productions were to enjoy public success on a scale never accorded to Craig — was one of many directors whose theories were transformed by Craig's innovations. This prodigious man, whose influence was profound and world-wide, was frustrated in many of his projects and saw comparatively little of his work realised in the theatre, but

* I am quoting from Janet Leeper's excellent King Penguin book on Edward Gordon Craig, to which I would refer everyone interested in this genius of the theatre.

Edward Gordon Craig: part of a scene-model for
Hamlet (Act II, Scene II) Moscow Art Theatre, 1910.
From a negative in the collection of Edward Craig

did, nevertheless, collaborate with some of the major figures of his time. Stanislavsky invited him to work at the Moscow Art Theatre and his production there of *Hamlet* was considered one of the most significant events in modern theatre history. He designed an ill-fated production of *Electra* for Eleonora Duse and productions at the Abbey Theatre in Dublin for W. B. Yeats, who was later to lecture on the work of Craig and Reinhardt in America. In Berlin in 1905 Craig met Isadora Duncan and recognised in her a fellow-revolutionary and together they crusaded for a new aesthetic in stage production and design. It is fascinating to contemplate these two visionaries travelling about Europe together; Craig's theories were profoundly to influence the theatre of the future.

Much has been written about Craig, and of his work and life, and even without ever having seen a Craig-designed production (how many people living *can* claim to have?) it is possible to recognise his importance in the evolution of modern stage-design. It comes as a shock to find among the eulogies to his genius the occasional attack on the impracticability of his designs, his lack of practical knowledge of scene-building and his inability to translate his designs into actual materials. Stanislavsky himself, while full of praise for the screens invented by Craig for his production of *Hamlet* at the Moscow Art Theatre, speaks of the difficulty encountered in keeping the large screens from falling. Mordecai Gorelik (in his *New Theatre For Old*) writes: 'At the final rehearsal, just as the audience was entering the theatre, the screens fell, breaking frames and tearing canvas all over the stage. The curtain, which Craig had intended to keep unused throughout the performance, had to be lowered and used

Edward Gordon Craig: Scene-model for *Hamlet*
(Act V, Scene II) Moscow Art Theatre, 1910.
From a negative in the collection of Edward Craig

all through the performance to cover scene shifts.'

Craig is accused by his critics of being a dreamer. There are numerous instances in the history of art where one finds the visionary showing the way - in a comparatively small body of work - for followers to whom it falls to realise, in their own creations, the full potential of the original discovery.

In retrospect we recognise the significance of Craig whose work and ideas were, with a few others, to bring about a renaissance in theatre design and production. His basic principles have nourished designers for sixty years, and there is abundant evidence in the theatre today of the lasting extent of his influence.

A postscript may be added: by a strange coincidence, as the above was being written, the

Jan Brazoa: Setting for *Parsifal* (Wagner)
Royal Opera House, Stockholm, 1963.
Photo: Enar Merkel Rydberg

news came of Craig's death in the South of France, where he had lived in retirement, outliving by generations his own epoch. Some years ago, a friend of the writer's, who happened to live in the same village, called on Craig and asked him to autograph a book on his (Craig's) work which was to be sent on to me. Wishing me well in my work he added the warning *'and don't compromise'*. He was an idealist, and certainly a dreamer, but one to heed. If we study the extraordinarily rich panorama of experiment in new scenic techniques during the first three decades of this century, we see that a great deal of contemporary stage design continues to explore the highly original theories and techniques evolved during this period.

Consider the wide range of styles to emerge during this turbulently creative time of scenic reform: the Symbolism of Craig and Appia, which was a reaction to various forms of Naturalism; Constructivism, making its first unpopular appearance in Tsarist Russia as early as 1911, and later becoming the scenic form for great director-designers such as Tairov and Meyerhold in that country (but finding advocates in the other countries of Europe and in America); the Painters' Theatre, inspired by the productions of Diaghilev for the Ballets Russes; the Expressionism of the Epic Theatre of Piscator and, later, Brecht in Germany. These together with Cubism, Vorticism and Futurism are some (but not all) of the major influences on a theatre constantly receptive to new ideas and mutations of seemingly opposing attitudes.

We might recall, also, some of the technical devices used for the first time, or re-discovered from a study of theatre history, and much in evidence today: the steeply raked stage; light-projections; revolving, sinking and sliding stages; cinematic projections; photo-montage; the use of unconventional materials in the design; the re-introduction of the forestage as a factor in breaking the Proscenium Barrier between audience and performers. These and many other innovations of the period are very much part of the vocabulary of the stage-designer of today.

More important, however, than merely employing many of the *techniques* of Symbolism and Constructivism is a return in *spirit* to these

Josef Svoboda : Setting for *Hamlet* (Shakespeare)
National Theatre of Belgium, Brussels, 1965.
Photo : Jaromir Svoboda

A design which, while highly original, displays strong affinities with the work of the early Russian Constructivists. The revival of interest in the experiments of such designer/directors as Mayerhold and Tairov has produced a School of designers termed Neo-Constructivist.

styles. In particular, a re-appraisal of the aesthetic of Constructivism appears to inform the work of certain designers, and the result is a form of neo-Constructivism.

The radical change in the concept of stage-design which came about with the introduction of Naturalism and Symbolism coincided with the invention of electric stage-lighting.

Although the first recorded use of electric lighting on the stage dates from as early as 1846, when an arc light was used at the Paris

Opéra to create the illusionistic effect of the sun shining in the sky, it was not until such designers as Craig and Appia began to consider stage lighting as a positive creative and emotive part of scene design that the potential of this important new element began to be realised. In ideal theatre conditions the lighting specialist has come to be considered an essential contributor to the stage entity. In less ideal conditions, particularly in much of commercial theatre, designer and director may work in close collaboration yet find that the production is not lit until the final rehearsals, when there will be insufficient time for finding the maximum creative part the lighting can play in revealing the full potential of setting and production. (And this is not to mention the often inadequate time allowed for the rehearsal of lighting cues and special effects.)

As we have seen, the revolutionary attitude at the turn of the century to the stage designer's role was followed by a positive renaissance of theatre design. In a comparatively short span of time a new understanding of the tremendous potential of the medium had been grasped and explored. This period, rich in experiment, was followed by a decade, prior to the Second World War, when designers appeared to be consolidating the achievements of their predecessors. In the feverish climate of these years so much had been quickly assimilated into the vocabulary of stage language that designers needed a spell — provided, ironically, by the war years — in which to take stock. Scene design, in many areas still reactionary and clinging nostalgically to old traditions, became, in the hands of others, assertive and dominant. As we will see later, certain scenic forms had been tried but insufficiently exploited and would be re-discovered by a new generation of post-war designers.

Early Russian Constructivist Setting

It is ironical that, regardless of the achievements of the influential school of Russian painter-designers, and, later, the experimental and highly original settings devised by such post-Revolution designers as Ryndin and Tischler, the Russian stage has reverted to essays in the Naturalistic and Romantic traditions.
In visits to Western Europe the Moscow Arts Theatre and the Bolshoi and Kirov Ballet Companies have been seen all too frequently in décors so reactionary and uninspired as to seem totally unworthy of the artistry of the performers.

We have seen that Diaghilev revolutionised the ballet stage and that his principles led to a highly successful formula for producing works of great visual impact and beauty.

By re-asserting the importance of the painter in the theatre Diaghilev discovered an incredibly rich potential, which he himself exploited to the full and which continues today in the scenic style loosely termed Painters' Theatre. Not only the décors of the Ballets Russes, but a great many created since, resort technically to the illusionistic tradition of the Romantic Theatre in the use of painted backdrops, gauzes and wings. On the ballet stage it is a scenic form dictated largely by the choreographic need for the maximum stage space for movement. It is also, of course, the framework for ballets being created today — although many designers are endeavouring to devise more varied scenic structures. Among certain contemporary designers the aim has been to bring something of the scenic materials and styles more often associated with the dramatic theatre to the ballet stage.

One of the hazards of attempting to carve up the volume of the stage space into more interesting patterns is that the functional need for a large uncluttered area of dance space will not be met. If the demands made on the ballet designer to keep the main area of the stage free for dancers have tended to restrict the search for new scenic forms, it must be admitted that, on the credit side, he has been helped by the lyrical nature of the medium to come to terms with many of the scenic conventions rejected long ago by designers working for the straight theatre. The majority of Diaghilev's artists tended to treat the stage as a large canvas and

Ralph Koltai: Setting for *Cul de Sac* (Whelan/Morrice)
Ballet Rambert, Sadlers Wells Theatre, London, 1965.
Photo: Anthony Crickmay

Alexandre Benois: Set Design for *Petrouchka*
(Stravinsky/Fokine)
Théâtre du Châtelet, Paris, 1911.
Photo: Roy Round

were often content to have their designs interpreted simply (and even, at times, naively) in
terms of backdrops and 'wings' or 'flats'. This
was done to retain as nearly as possible the
two-dimensional quality of a painting. There
are, of course, notable exceptions. An early
example is Alexandre Benois' décor for
Petrouchka in 1911 (see fig. 11) and a later one,
the setting devised by the Constructivists Naum
Gabo and Antoine Pevsner for *La Chatte* – a
ballet commissioned by Diaghilev in 1927.
During the reign of Diaghilev as Artistic
Director and sole arbiter of the Ballets Russes

most of the leading painters of the then all important School of Paris were commissioned to create designs for his company. It is interesting to note that Diaghilev (who by no means confined his search for new designers to the Parisian scene) inexplicably overlooked the genius of Paul Klee, whose poetic imagery and lyricism would seem to have been ideally suited to the medium of ballet. The list of painters who *did* contribute to the ballet theatre of this period reads like a Painters' Who's Who! Picasso, Braque, Derain, Léger, Laurencin, Rouault, Picabia and Pruna are some of the artists who created designs for the Ballets Russes.

With the death of Diaghilev the great forces he had assembled were scattered all over the world. Members of the company dispersed, and it was not until three years later that the first attempt was made (by Colonel de Basil) to re-form a company which would perform not only new works but preserve many of the ballets created under the aegis of Diaghilev. With the formation of rival companies to de Basil's Ballets Russes, new opportunities occurred for easel-painters to work in the theatre. Artists were, by now, quick to see in the theatre a stimulating extension of their activity as painters. More and more were drawn into the theatre and created settings not only for ballets but for plays and operas.

Writing of the ballet theatre at this time George Amberg (in his book *Art in Modern Ballet*) says: 'For ballet design it was decidedly a most profitable development. The artists, for the most part distinguished easel-painters, created with an unrestrained disregard for stage mechanics and dance requirements never before permitted them in the modern theatre. They established the *supremacy of the scenic image* as an

uncontested principle before anybody became aware of its basic fallacy'. The italics are mine, and I think in this phrase is summed up the ultimate consequence of Diaghilev's practice of commissioning designs from the greatest easel-painters of the day. The original premise, vindicated in so many of the earlier productions — to create a work in which each element formed a perfect complement to the other components — was frequently lost when the balance became upset by the use of décors too powerfully beautiful in themselves.

Directors (and even, later, choreographers) began to suspect that the ballet stage was becoming a sacred show-case for artists, and that scenery as visually compelling and self-sufficient had little or no place in the straight theatre. Quite rightly, the dramatic theatre was demanding — and producing — its own scenic forms. In Europe and America the possibilities shown and hinted at by the variety of deeply questioning experiments carried out in the Russian theatre prior to, and just after, the Revolution were causing designers to explore new paths in a search for style; a style which would become one with the new wave of producers' aims in re-interpreting the classics, and in staging the new plays being written.

If we remember that at this time it was barely forty years since such pioneers of modern stage design as Antoine, Stanislavsky, Appia and Craig had begun to change the face of the world's stages, we can appreciate that to producers and designers alike the new potential must have seemed challenging and limitless. Directors (such as Tairov, Piscator, Brecht and Copeau) emerged who were further to enlarge the vocabulary of stage production — and in doing so they proved also to be *scenic* reformers, for their methods inspired the invention of original scenic devices and innovations of staging and interpretation.

It should, perhaps, be pointed out that I am speaking only of the serious, creative theatre which then, as it is today, was very much the minority theatre. By far the larger proportion of theatre production and design was either frankly bad, superficially modern (and pretty half-baked) or in the tradition of outmoded Naturalism.

The important thing is that by this time directors and audiences were coming to accept the designer as a vital and influential link in the total collaboration. Designers, for their part, were beginning to take stock of the staggering advances made in the whole concept of design, which up till 1900 had developed gradually; and the major changes, once established, had remained the accepted convention for long periods. Not only were designers imposing new pictorial disciplines and attempting in many ways to provide the perfect complement to the style of writing, production and acting, but they were also assessing and consolidating the ground covered by such brilliant innovators as Tairov, Meyerhold, Reinhardt and Artaud. Some years later there emerged from this scene a number of painter-designers whose work showed a common interest in the return to a more romantic idiom. Pavel Tchelichew, Eugene Berman and Christian Bérard were among the most original of these neo-Romantics, whose respective styles had a marked effect on a whole generation of designers — particularly in America (Tchelichew and Berman were both Russian émigrés to America) and in England and France. Bérard, in Paris a veritable High Priest of taste, created highly evocative settings of astonishing purity and economy. His style, elusive but always theatri-

Christian Bérard: Costume designs for *Symphonie Fantastique* (Berlioz/Massine)
The Royal Opera House, Covent Garden, 1936.
Photo: W. Delafield Cook

Christian Bérard: Set design for *Les Fourberies de Scapin* (Molière)
Photo: W. Delafield Cook

Eugene Berman: Set design for *Danses Concertantes*
(Balanchine/Stravinsky)
New York City Center, 1944.
Photo: Gift of the Committee for the Dance Collection,
New York Public Library

cally sure, was born of infallible judgement and a masterly ability to create a convincing distillation of a period, mood or place. The actual sketches by Bérard do little to convey the magic spell he was able to cast upon a stage — and this by the use of unremarkable, conventional scenic materials. His influence on post-war designers was extensive, and in England, for example, the settings and costumes of Sophie Fedorovitch — although personal in style — owe much to his purity of vision.

The painter Eugene Berman, who has designed a large body of work for the theatre has always been much concerned with the romance of ruins. This imagery, in the hands of a draughts-

Antoni Clavé: Set design for *Devil en 24 Heures*
(Thiriet/Petit)
Théâtre de l'Empire, Paris, 1953.
Photo: W. Delafield Cook

man and artist of Berman's calibre, contained a poetic and deeply meaningful view of life, but it was, in the 1940's, exploited by Hollywood and a host of imitators. Designs of this period frequently express the nostalgic, melancholy view of the ruined splendour of a past epoch, which suited exactly the post-war mood of regret for a world lost forever. Berman's settings represent far more than a pastiche of the Renaissance and Baroque; they are an attempt to reinstate — in the rigidly architectural themes of his scene designs — the order of Classicism. In a debased form the fake-nostalgic image of ruins became one of the most monotonous pictorial clichés in stage and film design of the post-war years. Tchelichew, a fine, mystical painter, designed several ballets of almost classical severity – though, nevertheless, they belong aesthetically to the neo-Romantic School.

Then, into the post-war theatre, there exploded like a dazzling firework display the vivid scenic audacities of the painter Antoni Clavé. His designs (created mostly for the Ballets de Roland Petit) embody the true Catalan spirit of plastic and pictorial theatricality. Clavé, besides bringing his highly individual and very painterly style and imagery into the theatre, also found new solutions to the problem of filling out the stagespace by deploying the scenic masses in daring and unconventional juxtaposition. These designs, by turn dramatic and witty, reflected precisely the spirit of the choreography and combine an unusual painterliness with an astute awareness of the function of ballet scenery.

Reacting to the austerity of the war years, designers for a time created highly decorative, elaborate and elegant settings which a spectacle-starved public appeared to need ·and demand. This was especially the case in the English theatre. If one compares the productions of the Shakespeare Memorial Theatre, Stratford-on-Avon from 1945 to 1955 with recent productions at this theatre, one is made aware of the stylistic change that has come about in the past decade. The former period is characterised by settings of pictorial beauty executed by somewhat conventional means and displaying a lavish use of colour and materials. Designers were clearly intent on stressing the ornamental, the romantic and the heraldic aspects of the plays. The result was a theatricality which – although it pleased audiences and directors for a time – ultimately brought about the reaction of a more austere scenic approach, with the emphasis shifting to a new (at times obsessive) interest in the texture of materials, and a belated interest in Constructivist principles and techniques.

Recovering from the effects of the Second World War, the theatre took immediate refuge in various forms of escapist entertainment Revivals of well-tried successes, elegant comedies and worthy productions of the classics ensued. The theatre was basking in a late Romantic twilight; but it was suspected that the theatre of the future would be different. In England the new playwrights — as yet unheralded — were preparing for an onslaught on the rigid monopolies of the commercial theatre; the plays of Osborne, Wesker, Behan, Delaney, among others, and the irreverent productions, which rapidly moved West from Joan Littlewood's Theatre Workshop, were manifestations of a changing theatrical climate. Even earlier than these important arrivals on the English scene, playwrights as original as Tenessee Williams and Arthur Miller had begun to influence the drama in America. Their plays with their clear-cut stage directions stipulating the need for a composite set, were an example of a dramatic form requiring new scenic solutions. In the theatre today — and the dramatic theatre particularly — emphasis has come to be placed on a simplicity that allows for the greatest power of suggestion. This visual austerity is frequently tied to a form of production which plays down the setting and attempts to concentrate the attention of the audience on the actor and, as critics never tire of saying, 'allows the play to speak for itself'.

Audiences have become conditioned to tonal décors often totally lacking in colour, and this tonal setting has become ubiquitous. The safe formula of a monotone set with colour reserved for the costumes has become one of the most overworked scenic clichés of the theatre today. This mistrust, on the part of many directors, of a more eloquent scenic image is a reaction against the pictorial excesses and often purely decorative and show-stealing décors which preceded, and to a large extent brought about, this trend. It is a reaction which has often produced settings over-simplified to the point of dullness and vacuity. This is a far cry from the vibrating and meaningful simplicities of designs by Craig or Appia. It is far more subtle and enriching to the end result to find a perfect balance between the dramatic and visual components, than to make all else *subservient* to the performer. No intelligent designer misunderstands the central importance of the actor and the play, but it must by now be understood that a designer's function is to *add* to the total impact on the senses of an audience.

In recent years a bizarre division has been made by critics, and even by designers themselves, between painter-designers and constructivist-designers. A school of designers has come into prominence which dispenses with certain, though not all, of the usual materials associated with the making of stage scenery. 'Cheap scene paint' is eschewed and many materials new in the building of scenery are used instead. Emphasis is placed on 'real' materials — iron, steel and aluminium — and much use made of new materials — polystyrene, fibre-glass and other plastics — and the texture of the materials attains a vital importance. Designers working in this idiom frequently achieve visual eloquence in the construction of a setting employing such materials, and it is certainly true that a constructivist setting has at least one distinct advantage over a set made of painted canvas and wood flats and back-drops: it is infinitely easier to light. Any three-dimensional object lit obliquely will, by virtue of the light and shade, describe a tangible form. The forms embodied in a painted design have their own laws of light and shade and can be easily contradicted and distorted by stage lighting.

'Comparisons are odorous', as that forthright lady of the theatre, Mrs Malaprop, wisely remarks; and the truth is, of course, that the division between painted and constructivist sets is an arbitrary one which has meaning for one designer but not for another. One will choose to work strictly within the limits of a given idiom, another will find that a combination of techniques can be made to 'work'. It remains a matter of instinct whether or not to adhere dogmatically to any given aesthetic standpoint.

A danger in the obsessive interest in new materials ('texturology') seems to be that they are often employed neither evocatively nor because their use springs from the very nature of the play itself, but for their own sake. Thus one sometimes finds a work mounted in materials in which the designer has a predetermined interest, but which are utterly unsuitable for the piece. Used intelligently and subtly, of course, the designer should feel free to incorporate any new materials he chooses into his design. But it becomes prodigal to build sets in iron and steel if they can be built lightly and cheaply in wood and canvas and have the same meaning in the total stage picture. I recall, as an illustration, a recent production where the expensive 'flats' and cut-outs were constructed in heavy metal and then *covered in scene-canvas*. They proved difficult and unwieldy (and possibly dangerous) in practice.

On the other hand tubular metal scaffolding

used to construct rostra and to make various forms of framework, although initially more expensive than wood, can be made up and dismantled very quickly.

In today's wide range of scenic styles there exists a kind of heightened realism which, by virtue of selecting certain realistic objects and background material in compounding the set, can surpass mere naturalism.

Time and again we see a designer working in terms of an *apparently* straightforward representation of a recognisable place, which attains its extra degree of potency through the meaningful stresses and emphases given to the realistic *components* in the design.

Designers have become aware that many of the laws governing other more abstract forms of art, in which for example, questions of the thrust, rhythm and balance become paramount, can be applied to a primarily conventional design. In this way it is possible to create a more dynamic form of realism.

As we find in assessing the quality of a work of art, certain criteria remain applicable, whatever the particular idiom to which the work belongs. We immediately recognise such things as good proportion, draughtsmanship, rhythmic design, colour harmony and true use of materials and knowledge of the medium. The designer may arrive at these things analytically, but the audience senses them intuitively.

Thus we begin to see that all the dull, indifferent design that accompanies so much 'realistic' drama could have been treated imaginatively and become 'good design'. Critics have spoken of 'scenery which is made to act'. All scenery acts – some scenery acts well, some badly.

Jo Mielziner: Set design for *Death of a Salesman*
(Miller)
Morosco Theatre, New York, 1949.
Photo: Peter A. Juley and Son

The Semi-permanent Set

The advantages of the semi-permanent set are manifold: it is primarily a technical means of enabling a production requiring frequent changes of place or atmosphere to be effected with minor changes to the permanent architectural frame. The semi-permanent set, which is the invention of no single school of designers, has been evolved and developed to its present ubiquitously important place in the modern theatre by the continuous exploration of its usefulness by designers in the present century. An audience, once aware that the larger pictorial framework of the environment is *permanent*, whatever changes may occur within that structure, is enabled to relax its visual attention to the mechanics of scene-changes. The very permanence of the main structural scenic elements induces a conviction and belief on the part of the audience, conditioned in this way to the permanent nature of the play's environment; and thus they will concentrate more easily on the performers and the dramatic content. An audience visually engaged by a totally new stage picture with every scene-change – even if the visual senses are being stimulated – is unable to give the same attention to other elements of the production. The degree of changing pictorial eloquence in a production is a problem to be resolved by designer and director, and will be governed by the very nature of the work being produced. In principle the greater the work and its dramatic content, the greater will be the need for visual restraint.

Ralph Koltai: Variable setting for *The Jew of Malta* (Marlowe)
Royal Shakespeare Company, Aldwych Theatre, London, 1964.

This contemporary set design pays obvious homage to Craig, whose ideas have been grasped and realised in practical terms by succeeding generations.

David Hockney: Setting for *Ubu Roi* (Jarry)
The Royal Court Theatre, London, 1966.
Photo: Dominic

The Painter's Role in the Theatre

In the past two decades painting has developed along paths so non-figurative that directors have refused to see any way in which this more abstract form of art could be allied to stage design. The theatre, formerly a most valid and aesthetically rewarding extension of a painter's activity, as we have seen from the Diaghilev and post-Diaghilev eras, has become almost totally divorced from the mainstream of modern art. A few timid experiments, a certain amount of borrowing here and there to make a pastiche of a painter's style, and the gulf in spirit and interrelation between the two media widens

42

Kenneth Rowell: Set design for *Bluebeard*
(Offenbach/Meilhac/Halóvy)
Sadlers Wells Opera, 1966.
Photo: W. Delafield Cook

Even when a new kind of figurative painting
appeared a few years ago under the label of
Pop Art, few of the leading exponents was
encouraged to bring their particular vision to
the theatre; exceptions were Robert Rauchen-
berg, who designed several ballets for the Merce
Cunningham Company in America and, in England, David Hockney's designs for *Ubu Roi*.
Painters today are, generally speaking, un-
interested in the theatre for the simple reason
that when they are lured there as spectators they
are, more often than not, confronted with what
they consider to be out-moded visual imagery.

John Piper: Set design for *The Turn of the Screw*
(Britten/Myfanwy Piper)
The English Opera Group, 1954.
Photo: W. Delafield Cook

John Piper: Set design for *Don Giovanni*
(Mozart/da Ponte)
Glyndebourne, 1951.
Photo: W. Delafield Cook

The theatre, formerly so receptive to the nourishing influences of painting and sculpture, is inundated with nostalgic, romantic décors resorting to all the old tricks of false perspective and trompe-l'oeil painting.

One hears it claimed in defence of scenery of this kind that it 'suits the work', but how often we see a production of an opera or classical ballet which could be made vastly more alive and meaningful by some new visual interpretation. The sad fact is that the percentage of really imaginative designers is lamentably small in the total body of theatre production. Audiences and, alas, producers, feel all too content and secure in the woolly framework of turgidly romantic settings. This is not at all to deny the need for a Romantic décor with which to frame an essentially Romantic work; but good design, draughtsmanship and imagination could enliven many a setting even in the Decorative/Romantic style which has become devitalised through an over-zealous attempt to re-construct a period. The need is to *re-interpret*, rather than re-construct — and this is something a painter is often able to accomplish with great conviction; and how many abstract and near-abstract ballets are created which could be matched by the cool, pure beauty of a contemporary painter or sculptor's style.

There are many artists today who would welcome the opportunity to collaborate on a production, as painters did so successfully under the aegis of Diaghilev and, as occasionally but all too seldom, they still do.

Although it must be admitted that much modern art is of a purity and in an idiom that would make it extremely difficult to relate to specific theatre works, there remains the fact that the equipment and vision of a painter is very different to that of the professional stage designer.

Teo Otto: Set design for *Saint Joan of the Stockyards* (Brecht)
Frankfurt am Main Municipal Theatres, 1963.
Photo: Ursula Seitz

Provided a painter is prepared to become acquainted with the very special technical problems of the medium and to come to understand the limitations and potential of the area or volume within the proscenium arch, it is very probable that he will be stimulated by the opportunity to express himself in another medium and the theatre will be enriched by the collaboration.

Opera Design

The operatic stage is dominated to a far larger degree than either the dramatic or balletic theatre by works created in the 18th and 19th Centuries. The conservative would have it that these operas belong so much to their period that any attempt to 'modernise' them courts disaster. Exceptions are made in the case of a work as timeless as, say, *The Magic Flute* which has been subjected to the widest range of interpretation.

The operas of Wagner are an instance of works originally conceived in a Romantic-Naturalistic idiom, which are now generally produced in a more stylised way, the extreme example being the symbolic productions by Wieland Wagner at Bayreuth.

It is interesting to note that many of Adolphe Appia's experiments in evolving a three-dimensional form of setting in which the actor was visually integrated were for Wagnerian operas (Appia designed *Tristan and Isolde* at the Scala Theatre, Milan in 1923 with Toscanini conducting, and *The Rheingold* and *The Valkyrie* at the Basel Stadt Theater in 1924). The predominance in the repertory of 'period' pieces means that opera houses remain strongholds of Baroque and Romantic design. Yet it is perfectly possible, as we have seen, for an imaginative and serious designer to create stage pictures which distil the essence of a particular time/place and are, at the same time, functional in terms of the director's needs and embody the elements of *good design*.

Unfortunately, what we too often tend to get are cumbersome, ill-proportioned replicas of the ornate Naturalism belonging to the late 19th Century. The quintessence of such staging, with its laboured attention to superfluous detail, is found in the currently ubiquitous Italian *Verismo* style. This, far from capturing the living spirit of a period, sets before the audience an elderly picture-postcard likeness of the scene; audiences and critics alike are seduced by opulence, false perspective and sentimental pictorial references to the past. Aesthetics aside, this heavy, un-manoeuverable scenery often serves the work badly in that, because of elaborate scene-changes, which are by no means always 'interval-changes', the dramatic line is broken and the audience's attention lost. Opera, at its greatest one of the most richly rewarding experiences in the theatre is, on one hand, in danger of becoming a museum of 19th Century art and, on the other, a powerful means of attracting vast audiences to the theatre. Music perhaps makes the most *direct* appeal to the sense. If producers of opera can ensure that the works are kept alive by interpreting them in terms acceptable to modern audiences and at the same time retain the essential musical greatness and dramatic spirit of the originals, the future of opera is assured. It is in this question of re-vitalising and making meaningful the production that the designer can play such an important role. However great and profound the literary, musical or choreographic content of a work, the theatre remains a *visual experience* as well.

John Bury: Setting for *Moses and Aaron* (Schönberg)
The Royal Opera House, Covent Garden, 1966.

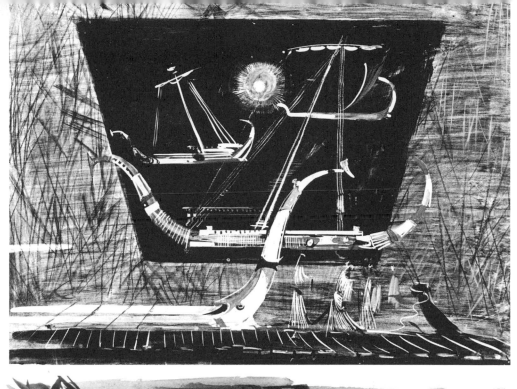

Contrasts in Swedish Opera Design
These three settings derive from distinctly different
scenic styles: (a) Painterly/Illusionist (b) Constructivist (c) Architectural.

Birger Bergling: Setting for *The Rake's Progress*
(Stravinsky/Auden/Kallman)
Royal Opera, Stockholm, 1961.
Photo: Enar Merkel Rydberg

Opposite:
Carl Johan Stroem: Setting for *Tristan and Isolde*
(Wagner)
Royal Opera, Stockholm, 1966.
Photo: Enar Merkel Rydberg

Opposite:
Helge Refu: Setting for *Don Carlos* (Verdi/Méry/
du Locle)
Royal Opera, Stockholm, 1950.
Photo: Enar Merkel Rydberg

54

Stage design changes when new theatre forms emerge. The Berliner Ensemble evolved not only a new technique in staging the epic plays of Bertolt Brecht but a scenic style to suit them; and so completely integrated is the acting with all the scenic elements that the two seem indivisible.

The Epic Theatre devised by Piscator (his celebrated production of *The Good Soldier Schweik* being a landmark in modern German theatre history) and later developed by Brecht had a profound effect on European and American left-wing theatre in the 1930s. In his book *New Theatres for Old* (published by Dennis Dobson) Mordecai Gorelik has said: 'The Symbolist thesis is that production must build up an emotional rapport between actors and audience (in the sense that actors are to enlist the heedless sympathy of the audience); and that the audience must suspend its more critical judgment. By now this view of production has spread so widely and been so little challenged that we have almost forgotten that it is only an opinion.'

It was by this means of *subjectively* appealing to the audience's emotional responses that the Symbolists Craig and Appia sought to establish a new relationship between all the theatrical elements and the audience. The most important challenge to this theory came with the Epic Theatre, which employed what has come to be known in English as the Alienation Technique of acting: wherein the motivation is to state *objectively* the situation of the protagonist and to disallow emotional involvement on the part of the audience. In this technique

Erik Skauronius: Setting for *The Masked Ball* (Verdi/Lindgren)
Royal Opera, Stockholm, 1958.
Photo: Enar Merkel Rydberg

Per Schwab: Setting for *After the Fall* (Miller)
National Theatre, Oslo, 1965.
Photo: Sturlason

Boris Aronson : Set design for *J. B* (MacLeish)
Anta Theatre, New York, 1959.
Photo : Robert Galbraith

Opposite:
David Hays : Setting for *All the Way Home* (Mosel)
Belasco Theatre, 1960.

Opposite:
David Hays : Setting for *Gideon* (Chayevsky)
Plymouth Theatre, New York, 1961.

the actor is required not to create the illusion of a realistic character, but to inform the audience of his personality and predicament in the drama. It is interesting to note that the English theatre came under the influence of this Brechtian technique and severely functional form of setting only in the post-war years and more especially after the visit of the Berliner Ensemble to England in 1956. The fundamental principle of this kind of setting is that every element of the design should be practical and non-illusory. It is indeed a form of dispassionate

realism wherein each object is intended to be realistically constructed rather than symbolised, and employed solely to serve and further the dramatic action. This technique has been used in a modified form for many contemporary theatre productions which do not strictly belong to the Epic Theatre – the semi-documentary musical *Oh What a Lovely War* is an example of the influence of Brecht's style on the English Theatre.

The dramatically important Theatre of the Absurd, which embraces playwrights as dif-

Sven Ericson: Set design for *Aniara*
(Blondahl/Londegren)
Royal Opera, Stockholm, 1959.
Photo: Enar Merkel Rydberg

K. Bubenik: Setting for *Electra*
(Richard Strauss/Hofmannsthal)
National Theatre, Prague, 1965.

ferent as Jarry, Beckett, Ionesco, Genet, Pinter and Albee, has produced no noticeably original scenic style, which in part may be explained by the fact that what is unconventional and seemingly erratic is heightened when seen in confrontation with the ordinary and commonplace.

It is always difficult to assess the work of one's own time before it has crystallised into a clearly recognisable style; we can only note the more obvious influences and trends. To attempt to predict the possible future direction of stage design would be hazardous and, almost certainly, inaccurate.

To the writer it seems that in the best contemporary design there is a new confidence and freedom in breaking down stylistic barriers and in assuming the right to make full use of past and present techniques. The principle guiding today's designer in the use of materials and techniques — regardless of the eclectic sources from which these may be drawn — is that all means of expression are valid if they achieve a greater dramatic effect, and in consequence add to the audience's understanding of the work. In the theatre the final criterion is whether an effect is used simply for its own sake (as a designer's or producer's conceit — and sometimes as such used deliberately to disguise inherent dramatic weaknesses) or to better express the inner content and outer reality of the drama.

It should perhaps be noted that, in view of technological advances now being made, many designers feel they need the assistance of a creative engineer to translate their ideas mechanically, and thereby produce settings of greater mobility. It is perfectly conceivable that a resident engineer will become part of the production staff personnel in the theatre of the future.

No matter how international the language of an art form may appear to be, it inevitably becomes imbued with an imprint that identifies it with the country from which it springs. Thus, although certain stylistic tendencies may appear to belong not so much to one particular country but to a universally accepted style, I think we will find that the national characteristics of a country will condition the aesthetic handling of these forms and techniques. More obviously, one country may be associated with a certain kind of theatre production and will even come to be considered pre-eminent in that field. In England, for example, the standard of Shakespearean production and acting obviously rates high (especially in a world sense, since such companies as The Royal Shakespeare Company and The National Theatre Company have toured their productions extensively). Again, where but in America can we find such prodigious talent lavished on musicals, some of which (such as *West Side Story* and *Fiddler on the Roof*) seem not to belong precisely to this category but to achieve the qualities of folk opera? A further example of a country becoming identified with a theatre form is to be found in Germany, particularly in the Bayreuth productions of Wagner, with their accent on, strongly symbolic interpretation.

In choosing examples of the stage design of different countries one is faced with a vast body of work from which — for a book of this size — it is possible to show only an arbitrarily chosen cross-section.

Opposite:
Robert O'Hearn: Set designs for *Die Frau Ohne Schatten* (Richard Strauss/Hofmannsthal) The Metropolitan Opera, New York, 1966.

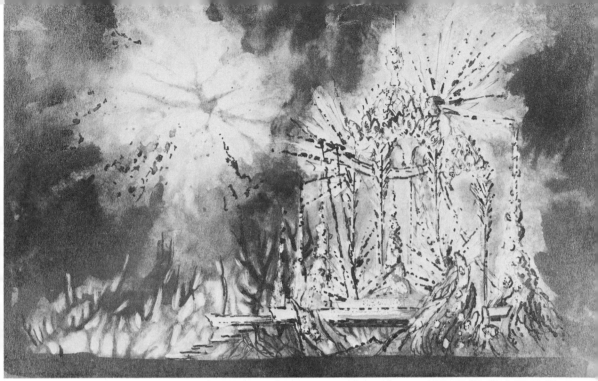

Cecil Beaton: design for a scene (Professor Higgins'
Study) in the film *My Fair Lady*, in which the agglomer-
ation of period detail makes a pungent and witty
environmental comment.

The American Musical

Some of the most original designs to be seen
in the American theatre are those created for
musicals — a theatre form into which so much
of the finest talent is canalised. It is not uncom-
mon to find first rate composers, writers and
choreographers, as well as designers, seeing in
this medium the greatest potential for expression. The episodic nature of most musicals, where
each act is usually composed of a number of
small scenes — and the dramatic necessity for
the action to move rapidly and smoothly from
one scene to the next — has brought about a
distinctive scenic style which is characterised
by a strict economy in the use of skeletal scenic
pieces (a kind of pictorial short-hand) allied

Irene Scharaff: Costume designs for *Hallelujah, Baby!*
(Styne/Comden/Green)
Martin Beck Theatre, New York, 1967.

Irene Scharaff's costume designs for *Hallelujah, Baby!*
interpret rather than reproduce the various periods
through which the play moves. The costumes not only
heighten the characterization but comment in their
own way on the emotions expressed by the actors and
succeed in underlining the wit and spirit of the music
and lyrics. The colour harmonies and line of the costumes are so carefully planned and co-ordinated that
they form a perfect foil to the settings. Scharaff's
costumes for *West Side Story* and many other productions have succeeded in creating costumes which
are at once contemporary in spirit but sufficiently
timeless to be more than a reflection of current fashions.

to a semipermanent or permanent form of
masking. Considerable technical expertise is
apparent in the manner in which trucks glide on
and off stage and scenic elements materialise and
dissolve with split-second timing. Settings of
this kind for such recent musicals as *Cabaret;
Sweet Charity; Mame; Hallulujah, Baby!*
convey with brilliant clarity and wit the mood/
time/place of each scene. With imagination and
ingenuity the designers have managed to
combine qualities of modern design (often
borrowing freely from the vocabulary of contemporary painting and sculpture) with an understanding of practical dramatic requirements.
These settings are invariably conceived in

Opposite :
Josef Svoboda : Setting for *The Makropulos Case*
(Janáček/Čapek)
National Theatre, Prague, 1965.
Photo : Jaromir Svoboda

Heightened Realism

Two settings by Josef Svoboda the Czech 'scenographer' whose experiments in applying comparatively 'alien' techniques — such as the multiple projection of photographic and filmed matter and the use of complex mechanically-operated scenic masses and rostra — has created a new conception of the stage in terms of space and light.

These techniques — while by no means new in themselves (Brecht and Piscator used these and other devices to heighten the dialectic of the play in their Epic Theatre) used by Svoboda with intensity and purpose attain a surprising form of heightened realism. Like all sound design the techniques are here employed to facilitate the action and express the fundamental ideas of the drama.

Opposite :
Josef Svoboda : Setting for *Osamene* (Slommcyynski)
National Theatre, Prague, 1961.
Photo : Jaromir Svoboda

conjunction with an equally imaginative lighting designer, and enormously benefit from this collaboration. At time scenery disappears almost entirely from the stage (or remains only as masking) and the lighting itself makes an eloquent visual statement. At its best and most creative, a kind of counterpoint exists between the scenery and the lighting with the two elements becoming interdependent.

An example is the cohesion between Boris Aronson's settings and Jean Rosenthal's lighting for *Cabaret*, a musical set in Berlin in 1929-1930. Sitting in the audience waiting for the performance to begin, the spectator is confronted (the house tabs being abolished) with a large tilted mirror in which a section of the audience is reflected. This in itself seems, and is, meaningful, and even before the play begins the audience is engaged. During the production, lights framing the black depths of the permanent surround flash on and off, momentarily blinding the audience, often facilitating rapid changes of scene to take place more effectively than in a black-out. Old-style footlights, denoting that we are in the Kit Kat Klub, emerge and disappear through the stage floor, and the mood of domestic drabness is contrasted with one of garish vulgarity throughout. Settings and lighting maintain a constant rapport in pungent theatrical terms.

If, in assessing the component parts that make up the final visual statement, we add the contribution to the stage of the costume designer (costume and scene design usually in the U.S.A. being regarded as separate departments and requiring individual designers), whose sense of style and colour will be integrated and complementary to the overall conception, we see the formula that produces a *mise-en-scene* of visual unity and theatrical potency.

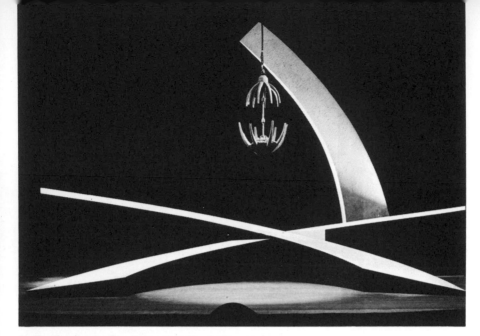

Cloffe: Setting for *The Pretenders* (Bucht/Ibsen)
Royal Opera, Stockholm, 1966. Photo: Enar Merkel Rydberg

Carl Frederik Reufersward: Setting for *Herr von Haucken*
(Blondahl/Bergman)
Royal Opera, Stockholm, 1965. Photo: Enar Merkel Rydberg

Teo Otto: Set design for *The Three-penny Opera*
(Weill/Brecht)
Frankfurt am Main Municipal Theatres, 1965. Photo: Ursula Seitz-Gray

H. W. Lennweit: Set design for *Lucifer and the Lord*
(Jean-Paul Sartre)
Frankfurt am Main Municipal Theatres, 1964. Photo: Ursula Seitz-Gray

The Future

The serious and creative theatre will not be content to remain in the moulds of the past, and the straight theatre (light years ahead of opera and ballet in evolving new forms) is treating boldly subjects previously thought to be the province of literature. We have become familiar with the somewhat glib terms coined to identify the new writing : The Theatre of the Absurd, The Theatre of Cruelty, etc. Many of those plays neither depend on nor require especially original settings or scenic devices (often, in fact, the reverse — as witness the conventional box-set used for the controversial *Who's Afraid of Virginia Woolf*); nevertheless designers are compelled to seek out the ideal framework for each play. To do this it is essential to comprehend the dynamics of the play, the rhythm of the production and the type and *degree* of visual statement required to bring about the most meaningful understanding of the work on the part of the audience, the actor and the producer.

With the intense competition provided by cinema and television, the theatre is, in a sense, fighting for its life — a fact of which the designer, no less than others in the theatre, is aware. As the language and technique of the cinema becomes more eloquent (and box-office takings increase) and as television continues to produce its own stars assured of vast audiences, the theatre looks to the future. The most powerful advantage the theatre will always possess over the other media is, of course, the attraction for an audience of being in the presence of a 'live' performance. Perhaps no less important for the audience is the intuitively-grasped fact that, as no two performances are ever identical, each one becomes a minor 'happening'.

The English theatre director Peter Hall has said : 'A vital theatre can only be produced by an audience which is drawn from all sections of the community'. The number of new theatres built in recent years in Europe and America (but also in other parts of the world) indicate that the theatre is far from being content to decline into a museum attracting a minority audience.

Designers are understandably impatient for new theatres which will liberate them from the handicaps of antiquated stages — whose bad sight lines mean that at least two thirds of the audience will have an oblique and distorted view of the stage. In the meantime it is found necessary to 'desecrate' the plaster and gilt stage boxes of the elegant but impossible Edwardian theatres by filling them with grim metal scaffolding on which to fix the much-needed extra lighting equipment. 'Aprons' are thrown out over the orchestra pits (nothing new in this: Meyerhold and Tairov both endeavoured in this way to break the Proscenium Barrier), and the complex problem of evolving a more flexible type of stage has never been so thoroughly investigated and debated. Unfortunately for many years yet designers will be forced to accept many of the limitations imposed by theatres belonging to a past epoch, while continuing to experiment and search for pictorial and theatrical awareness.

Per Schwab: Setting for *L'École des Femmes* (Molière)
National Theatre, Oslo, 1965.
Photo: Jan Schwarzott

Andreas Reinhardt: Setting for *Puntila* (Dessau)
State Opera, Berlin, 1966.
Photo: Marion Schöne

The variety of materials used in scenic design has greatly increased with the contemporary designer's interest in the potential of materials new in themselves, or new in this context. This pre-occupation with what we might call un-traditional materials — linked with a new concern for problems of building and staging — has evolved an organic quality of design central to the dramatic intentions of the production. Today it is not at all unusual to see sets incorporating the use of steel and other metals, plastics (such as polystyrene and fibre-glass), wire and other meshes, mirrors, and projections. This absorption with new textural effects — coupled with a builder's knowledge of methods of construction — has produced a school of designers who (although, stylistically, they are the descendants of such innovators as Craig and Appia, the Constructivists, the Cubists and the Realists) are giving the theatre — and more particularly the dramatic theatre — a valuable transfusion of new ideas. And the ideas seem, aesthetically, to express the time in which we live. Up to the 19th Century — and continuing today — stage scenery in physical terms has meant painted canvas; sometimes hanging loose as backdrops, cut cloths, legs, borders, etc., sometimes framed out with wood to make flats, wings and other set pieces. Sized canvas or papier maché, modelled over wood and wire armatures, is widely used to make such things as rostra, columns trees and rocks. Although inventive designers have exploited countless other materials, the staple of traditional scenery has remained canvas and scene paint.

The designs painted on the canvas have ranged over the whole gamut of art styles from *trompe l'oeil* to the most abstract of patterns. Indeed, most of the imagery of easel painters has ultimately found its way on to a stage – albeit often in a somewhat debased form.

While it is clear that designers should allow themselves complete freedom of choice in the use of new materials and methods, I think it is proper for them to acknowledge the usefulness of proven, traditional techniques, and important to realise that these are a valid and necessary part of the contemporary designer's equipment. Illusionistic effects, for instance, can sometimes be more perfectly achieved by conventional methods than with the use of infinitely more costly mechanistic apparatus in the form of hydraulic lifts, trucks, revolves, and sliding stages. There should be no boundaries of techniques and it can happen that apparently conflicting methods and materials may be combined and made entirely complementary to each other, provided the fusion is guided by an aesthetic sensibility.

What else governs a designer's choice of materials? In the absence of perfectly equipped stages and theatres, one is constantly forced to take into consideration the limitations of working in old badly-designed theatres, possessing antiquated technical equipment and often abysmally lacking in facilities for staging. Add to this the problem of designing for a repertory theatre when a set may have to be 'struck' very quickly in time for the next performance and the immense problem that most theatres have to contend with in the shortage of storage space, and it will be seen that the designs are conditioned to a large degree by the type of theatre (or theatres if a tour is involved) to which the production may have to be adapted.

To a modern designer – employing in his materials and techniques some of the by-products of engineering and modern science – these wicked old theatres with their bad sight-lines and crude scene-moving devices (to name but two of the bogies) seem impossibly out-moded.

And yet, while designers may dream of working on the splendidly planned and built stages which have come into being in recent years, these older theatres continue to be the scene of brilliant modern staging.

With great resourcefulness, designers have invented ways of transforming the stages of older theatres to such an extent that the audience is totally unaware of the technical difficulties involved. They have learnt (when necessary) to disguise or mask the rigid framework of the proscenium arch, and to extend the stage into the auditorium in the form of a forestage or apron.

Designers continually make great use of the convention of a permanent or semi-permanent set, in which minor changes or the shifting of focus within the established ambience are sufficient to evoke a change of time or place. Another device used extensively and often with great effectiveness is that of light projections. It is interesting to note that Gordon Craig was one of the first to use and guess at the future potential of this means of quickly altering the visual aspect and mood of a setting. The somewhat blurred and crude look of early projections has given way, with the invention of proficient new projectors, to images of much greater clarity and brilliance. The new equipment also permits a greater range of special effects such as the projection of moving, or advancing and receding, images.

With well-trained stage hands and mechanists, visual effects and entire scenes can be made to materialise and disappear with ease and split-second timing.

Kenneth Rowell : Set design for *Le Baiser de la Fée*
(Stravinsky/MacMillan)
The Royal Ballet, Covent Garden, 1960.

The success of any set that involves frequent
scene changes depends to a large degree on the
facility with which the changes are made. Until
such time as we have fully mechanised stages,
equipped with elevators, sliding stages, revolves
and the many mechanical devices we know are
possible, designers will still have to make do
and mend. They must attempt to achieve all the
effects of technical precision by careful planning and exercise of ingenuity – which to a
designer sometimes seems the first requisite in
theatre work.

Improvisation has always been one of the key
characteristics of the original theatre mind; the
Commedia del Arte players setting up a make-

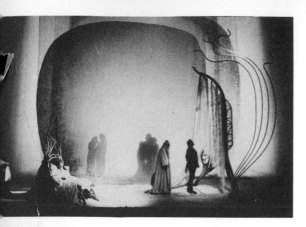

Rouben Ter-Arutunian : Setting for *Pelléas et Mélisande*
(Debussy)
Spoleto Festival, 1966.

shift stage of painted canvas and a few props were able to conjure up for their audience a believable world — a reality as convincing as a solidly-built façade.

Improvisation applies in every department of stage design : designer, costumier, prop-maker — all are required to use their ingenuity in the choice and handling of materials while the selection of the most suitable fabrics when the time comes for the designs to be translated is a vital and creative part of the work, over which much time is usually spent by the designer.

The set is essentially an artificially-created world, however much its creation may be based on a desire for total verisimilitude. And yet, in recent years, many designers have come to question this premise ; they want their sets built in the actual materials of the place they are representing.

There can be no dogmatic rule about this question of *real* versus *simulated ;* even a set which contrives to be quite representational will, in fact, represent a form of heightened realism. When John Bury built his 'meticulously pointed brick walls' for *Sparrers Can't Sing* he needed precisely that kind of solidly-built wall for his set to be valid and 'real'. When Oliver Smith designed his powerfully telling walls for *West Side Story* he seems to have had in mind some suggestion of the walls often depicted in Sienese paintings ; and, for his set, these were made of painted canvas.

But one can go further. Apparently alien techniques and materials can be mixed, and sometimes with great effect, as with the Czech designer, Josef Svoboda's, designs for the *Insect Play*, with their curious alchemy of huge tilted mirrors and the reflection of painted canvas on the stage floor. The result was a world of prismatic light and colour — dazzling, magical

Emmanuele Luzzati: Setting for *The Magic Flute*
(Mozart/Schikaneder)
Glyndebourne, 1963.
Photo: Guy Gravett

and a perfect vindication of the possibility of mixed techniques.

The inter-relation of the arts, which has become so marked in recent sculpture and painting, is beginning to be seen in stage settings; and in this fusion of painted, sculpted and architectural forms and the freedom to mix traditional and modern materials lies the modern designer's greatest potential.

If many stage designers are today, perhaps unconsciously, consolidating the discoveries of such visionaries as Craig, Diaghilev and others, this does not mean, of course, that they are not designing works of great originality. As I have indicated, new materials, new techniques – often arrived at by the dramatic requirements of the play or through some indication from the producer of his reading of the work – have produced settings of startlingly new beauty. Another innovation (often allied to this kind of design) is the use of electrically controlled mechanism of far greater complexity than any previously used in stage design. The engineer who specialises in solving mechanical problems, and in making models 'work', has become indispensible to many designers.

While undoubtedly useful in the rapid changing of one scene to another, mechanically propelled scenery and rostra can be used badly for their own sake. In some instances costly and complex machinery has been built into the stage with so little effect (and with comparatively so little help to the production) that the expense involved seems a prodigious waste and miscalculation. On the credit side, the use of mechanical apparatus to facilitate scene changes and the easy flow from one scenic image or stage picture to another has become a vital part of the stage designer's technical equipment. Audiences conditioned by film and television (media which present no problem in the effortless transposition from one scene to another) have come to expect a similar technical ease in the theatre. Directors now expect the time in effecting scene-changes to be cut to a minimum, in order to hold the audience's attention and to ensure the dramatic flow of a production. Scene changes which would previously have been made manually by stage hands are now more frequently effected by mechanical devices incorporated into the scenery. Designers — often with engineers working in close collaboration — have produced a great variety of ingenious solutions to the problem.

The designers I have been discussing above may be termed neo-Constructivists in that their work, stylistically speaking, has strong affinities with the original constructivists — although their work bears the stamp of recent technological developments and is concerned with a search for new scenic forms.

But another school of designers — which adheres more strictly to a painterliness and the continued use of traditional materials — continues to strive for an extension into the theatre of ideas being propounded in modern painting. It is not surprising, perhaps, that their work is more often seen in productions of ballet and opera than drama. The timeless ideal — and the one re-asserted by Diaghilev — for a perfect fusion of décor, music and movement continues to be the guiding factor of their work. Qualities of design, form and colour, frequently lacking in productions of plays, can be more easily absorbed into a theatrical form requiring less realism and greater fantasy.

With the building of theatres having stage facilities far superior to those found in the older buildings, the technique and aesthetic of stage design will, inevitably, change. Style and technique, as in any medium, are interdependent, and technical developments will tend to influence the future directions of stage design. In many modern continental theatres extensive use is made of in-built mechanical apparatus which permits fluid scene-changing and the use of multiple stage levels. Although splendidly-equipped stages of this kind are beginning to appear (in greater numbers in some countries than others — Germany, for instance, possesses a large number of new theatres) it will be the lot of the stage designer for many years to work in old, refurbished theatres.

The virtues and limitations of the open stage continue to be debated. To see a production of *Uncle Vanya* first on the open stage of the newly built theatre at Chichester in England and then transferred to the vastly different confines of the Old Vic Theatre in London enables one to assess the advantages and disadvantages of both stages.

A designer in one production, able to exploit the potential of a newly built theatre equipped with modern technical apparatus, may, in his next production, be forced to take into account the alarming variables and pitfalls of a provincial tour. But if, as it seems, the path is strewn with obstacles, it must also be said that in finding solutions to these problems and in experiencing the pleasure of making the designs an integral part of the play the designer is challenged and, to the stage-struck (be he interpretive or creative artist) nothing else ever offers exactly the same stimulus and, with hard work, sense of fulfilment.

The theatre is a collaborative art form in which each part must be considered in relation to the whole. To certain artists, a medium in which one is not wholly in charge is bound ultimately to prove unsatisfactory as a means of expression; stage-designing, in this sense, is an imperfect medium. In each production the balance alters: the visual statement, dominant in one type of production, will be subservient in another. The varying contribution a designer makes to a production depends on the total stage entity as envisaged by the director and the designer himself. The experienced designer has learnt to accept the limitations of the medium and acknowledge the ephemeral nature of a theatre production.

What, then, lures artists and designers to the theatre? Primarily, of course, the theatre itself, which — in spite of the limitations mentioned above — is a powerfully attractive world.

Two settings for the same play (John Osborne's *Inadmissable Evidence*) show identical placing of the vital components but reveal a different degree of visual statement regarding the plays' theme/place.

Opposite:
Per Schwab: Setting for *Inadmissable Evidence* (Osborne)
National Theatre, Oslo, 1965
Photo: Jan Schwarzott

Jocelyn Herbert: Setting for *Inadmissable Evidence* (Osborne)
The Royal Court Theatre, London, 1965.
Photo: Dominic

The well-known loneliness that attends the painter working in isolation in his studio for long periods is not known to the stage designer, the very nature of whose work guarantees that he is in constant touch with others involved on the project. This proves a stimulating and even necessary experience for artists of a certain temperament. It is an unfortunate fact that stage designers, more than others, are subject to changes of taste and fashion and a craving for new talent. Many a young designer has a success which lasts for a few years, during which his work is in great demand, only to find that one day he is without work in the theatre. For this is a vastly over-crowded profession, with the few art schools which have a department of stage design turning out a small stream of partly-trained young designers, often with marked and original talent. But to the stage-struck none of this will act as a deterrent — for there is a unique satisfaction in seeing one's work come alive on the large scale of the stage and with a guaranteed (one hopes) audience. Nor does the fact that designers, except for the very successful, are comparatively poorly paid prevent them from seeking work in the theatre.

Training

What is the best training for becoming a stage designer? There is no single answer, but a great deal that a student learns in a general art course will be of invaluable help in acquiring a technique. To come to appreciate the problems of design, form, line and colour, to acquire a sense of draughtsmanship, to learn to paint, all these provide the student with a technique which is an essential part of a stage designer's equipment. Add to this the fact that most art courses now embrace liberal studies, entailing a study of the History of Art, and it will be seen

82

that this provides a certain amount of sound basic training for the aspirant designer. Some art schools have departments of stage design with instruction by professional designers, and when there is a theatre attached to the school, useful practical experience can be gained. However, not all future stage designers arrive via the art schools, and particularly now, when so many stylistic changes are occurring in the theatre and sets are frequently created instead from a sound knowledge of building materials, lighting and techniques indigenous to the theatre. Many successful designers, in fact, have had no formal art training. The conclusion must be that there is no *specific* way of becoming a stage designer; it is largely a matter of the temperament of the individual and the idiom in which he intends to work that determines the means of entry into the theatre.

Production

In the initial stages, during preliminary discussions with the director, and whilst working on the actual designs and endeavouring to solve the inherent problem of style and the practical problem of staging, the designer finds it easy to sustain his interest and enthusiasm. However, the novice-designer soon learns that only a fraction of the total time spent on a production is occupied with making the original designs and/or models and working drawings; by far the longest time is taken up in the long, necessary grind of supervising the execution. Endless care and attention to detail are necessary to ensure that the designs are accurately interpreted. For, with the best will in the world, and even if the work is entrusted to highly skilled and experienced workers and technicians, the designs can be subtly (and sometimes, alas, grossly) distorted. Nothing takes the place of a personal relationship with the people interpreting the designs. To risk allowing work to be carried out without first making clear one's requirements – and this followed by constant supervision – is to store up disappointments for the time when the work is finally seen on the stage, by which time major alterations will be difficult. There are, also, the inevitable miscalculations to be taken care of, since no designs are ever entirely predictable in the end result, and adjustments are always necessary when the work is finally assembled.

The professional stage designer (if not the painter who makes an occasional excursion into the realm of the theatre) will in the course of his career be required to make settings descriptive of a great many periods and styles. He will scarcely have time to learn all he needs to know about the history of architecture and costume and about the potential of colour and form. This is a medium requiring at least a working knowledge of many subjects, among which I would also include an appreciation of the capabilities, or still better the technique, of stage-lighting. Even when, as generally happens today, the lighting is entrusted to a specialist, the designer is deeply concerned with the relation between the lighting and his designs. The theatre attracts and needs designers of vastly different kinds and, although the proportion of productions which get imaginative and creative designs is lamentably small, we should keep in mind the fact that a farce deserves a setting as good in its way as a classical drama. Good design and good craftsmanship can but serve the production and satisfy the designer's need for self-expression. It is important to think in terms of the theatre as a medium in which the designer, by illuminating the meaning of the play, is able to regard his contribution as a creative part of the whole.

Kenneth Rowell: Costume designs for *Bluebeard*
(Offenbach/Meilhac/Halévy)
Sadlers Wells Opera, 1966.

Costume Design

New scenic styles produce original attitudes to costume design; it is obvious that the use of certain materials, textures, shapes and rhythms inherent in a setting will need to be reflected in the costumes, and to achieve a complete unity of style the two need to be continually considered in relation to each other. There are two basic attitudes to the designing of period costumes: the first aims to provide designs which are accurate *re-creations* to some degree of authentic period clothes, and the other to *interpret* the particular period according to the contemporary aesthetic climate. But as with the setting, the interpretation of a period will be conditioned by the style and vision of the designer; each generation has a different conception of what a previous age was like and will stress certain aspects of that epoch and disregard others. It is in this selecting of what the designer considers the significant characteristics that the synthesis of a period is achieved. Of course it goes without saying that although it may seem easy, it is a difficult process involving taste and imagination and, initially, a genuine feeling for the period that produces a real interpretation of this kind. It is not sufficient to add a ruff or farthingale to modern dress, although in fact many designers have cleverly shown that period costumes can be interpreted in a contemporary spirit, and even deliberate anachronisms may be appropriate to a certain kind of play. Determining the *degree* of period authenticity becomes, as so often in this medium, a problem that is only resolved by considering the play itself, together with the producer's aims.

The best means of doing some research, to enable the designer to become familiar with a period, is to study paintings, illustrations and the decorative and literary arts of that period,

Yolande Sonnabend: Costume design for *Orfeo*
(Monteverdi/Striggio)
Sadlers Wells Opera, 1965.
Photo: Massie Clifford Ltd

Nicholas Georgiadis: Costume designs for *Romeo and Juliet* (Prokofiev/MacMillan)
The Royal Ballet, Covent Garden, 1965.
Photo: Anthony Crickmay

Alix Stone: Costume design for *The Mines of Sulphur* (Bennett/Cross) Sadlers Wells Opera, 1965.

the worst way is to become lost in textbooks dealing with historical costume.

Designers who comb the markets for pieces of *authentic* stuff create extra problems for the costumier (and incidentally for the wardrobe staff, who will be responsible for the maintenance of the costumes); and more often than not some object or piece of period materials, while beautiful in the hand, will be lost in the vastness of the theatre. Even in the re-creating of period clothes the stage has its own laws of what is theatrically true; just as a piece of 'real' antique furniture can sometimes appear less convincing than the artifact. As the Greeks preferred their actors to wear neither archaic costume nor modern dress but invented instead a style more appropriate to the drama, so many designers today attempt to imbue stage costumes with a timelessness that make them more interesting, and often easier, not only for the actor to wear, but also more meaningful in the stage picture.

During the present century designers have experimented ceaselessly in trying to invent theatrically effective costumes which, valid in that context, have no meaning outside the theatre. Costumes are often painted, sprayed, broken down and treated in other ways to make them at one with the setting.

It is axiomatic that certain colours induce certain emotions and, therefore, with regard to dressing an actor or groups of actors, colour should always be thought of emotively. Most designers have a grand colour plan in mind before they actually get all the designs down on paper; sometimes the *palette* of a production may suggest itself to producer and designer alike before they have established any other pictorial signposts.

A word here about the relationship of designer

and actor, dancer or singer. Even when the costume is conceived with the physique of the actor in mind, the designer must be prepared to adapt his design to the actor's temperament and needs. A certain amount of compromise is almost always inevitable, and, as every designer soon learns, actors can be stubborn and refuse to see why a certain aspect of the design may be vital to the overall conception of the play. Whenever possible it is essential to show the entire cast at the outset not only the costume but also the set designs, and to explain the pictorial style of the production and the reasons for this style. An actor is much more likely to be sympathetic to the designer's aims if he has had the total visual plan of the production explained to him, than if he arrives at his first fitting faced for the first time with the design of the costume he is to wear. Actors almost never have enough time to 'break a costume in' – to feel how they can use it to further the characterisation, and the dreaded costume parade, which is unnerving for all involved, inevitably reveals faults which were not apparent at the fittings. At this first assembling of the cast and their costumes the designer himself may be seeing the total costume for the first time. Later when they are seen against the setting for the first time there will be further surprises, both agreeable and depressing, and this is often the crucial time when patience must prevail on both sides. Like all other designers, I have experienced extremes of attitude, from the temperamental actress who caused all her costumes to be weighed so that she could tax me over the 'great weight' she had to 'drag around' and, by contrast, the actors, dancers and singers who, with their enthusiasm for the designs, make the theatre a uniquely satisfying medium in which to work.

Hollywood Musical: *The Great Ziegfeld*, 1937.

Designing for Television and Cinema

Hollywood Baroque: in the 1930's designers of
Hollywood musicals surpassed themselves in devising
settings of glittering extravagance. Created as a
palliative to the harsh realities of the depression it is
impossible not to admire a little these escapist fantasies
which are spectacular essays in the luxurious and
romantic. The vast scale of the settings derives in part
from the grandiose stage productions of Max
Reinhardt.

While a number of schools have courses in
theatre design, comparatively few offer special
instruction for the would-be television or
cinema designer, and many who are trained
as stage designers eventually gravitate to the
other media, finding that at least part of the
basic training they have had is applicable.
However it must be admitted that each of these
three media make distinctly different demands
on the designer or 'art director'. For instance
the student of stage design will find that, either
through the opportunities provided by the
school, or by some other means — perhaps by
working in repertory or with semi-professional

groups – he will be able to gain some first-hand experience of actual theatre conditions. It will be much more difficult whilst still a student to gain similar experience in either television studios or the film industry. Specialised training not being available it becomes a question of gaining some basic training as a draughtsman, acquiring at least some technique that will enable him to make designs, and working- and scale-drawings and then deciding to specialise in whatever the chosen field. Established professional designers rarely work in more than one medium even though many a stage designer would welcome the change to try his hand in the cinema, and vice versa. But the problems central to each are singular, and it takes years of experience in either to produce a designer with a strong technical grasp of the medium. What use is an understanding of *stage*-techniques to a film designer who will be concerned with totally different problems, whether he has to have sets built on the studio floor or to work on location?

Again, the kind of accuracy in the reproduction of architectural settings, the felicity of period detail necessary in creating cinematic backgrounds would be entirely wasted and out of place in the theatre. The brilliant 1919 German film *Dr Caligari*, which owed its success largely to the originality of its painter-designed Expressionist settings, was not apparently an idiom which cinema directors were prepared to explore further. Television design is in the main governed by the same aesthetic need for uncompromisingly realistic settings as the cinema. In cinema history the notable exceptions are the extravagantly fantastic settings created for the Hollywood musicals of the 1930s and 1940s. Later even musicals such as *West Side Story* demanded realistic or location sets. The inven-

Television design by Evan Hercules (BBC Television) showing section of a setting characteristic of the form of extreme naturalism demanded by a medium often primarily concerned with the re-creation – in precise terms – of identifiable places.

tiveness of most film-making today springs from brilliant and sophisticated new camera techniques and the director's personality rather than from any novelty in the actual settings. Federico Fellini, tried to redress the balance. All this indicates that the basic training to become a television or cinema designer may be only partly the same as that for the theatre designer. Having once acquired the rudiments of painting, draughtsmanship and a sense of history the need then is to become attached as quickly as possible to a television studio or a film company, where experience of the actual conditions in the particular medium is the only means of acquiring the specialised technique.

Glossary of technical terms

where usage differs, the American equivalent is shown in italics.

APRON or FORESTAGE	That part of the stage which extends into the auditorium beyond the proscenium arch or house curtain.
ARENA	An acting area totally or partly surrounded by the audience.
BACKCLOTH or BACKDROP	Scene-canvas (usually fire-proofed) battened at top and bottom to keep it taut. The seams of the cloth are sewn horizontally.
BACKING	A flat or cloth used behind door or window — or to otherwise mask part of the stage which should not be visible to the audience.
BARREL or BAR *PIPE*	A movable iron tube hung horizontally above the stage for carrying scenery and lighting equipment — can be moved vertically from stage level to grid level.
BATTEN (Scenic)	A length of timber (often 3 in. x 1 in.) slotted through backcloths at top and bottom.
BATTEN (Electrical) *BORDER LIGHT*	A horizontal trough divided into compartments, each carrying a lamp reflector and colour medium. Usually divided into 4 circuits and — as it is non-directional light — is used to give all-over diffused light on backcloth and borders, etc.
BOOK FLAT *TWO-FOLD FLAT*	Two flats hinged together so that they fold back to back.
BOOMERANG or BOOM *VERTICAL PIPE*	A vertical iron tube used to carry spot-lights positioned in the wings, — the main source of high sidelighting.
BORDER	A horizontal flat, un-battened canvas or narrow curtain hung parallel to the proscenium arch to mask scenery and lighting hung from the grid.
BOX SET	An enclosed setting representing the three walls and ceiling of a room.
BRACE	A support for a flat — extendable metal arm supports flat by screwing foot to stage floor or fixing by a weight.
BRAIL LINE *GUIDE LINE*	Rope or sash line for adjusting position of hanging scenery up and down stage.
CARPET CUT	A long narrow trap (parallel with footlights) at front of stage used to secure front of carpet or stage-cloth.
CENTRE LINE	A line bisecting stage from front to back. It should be shown on the ground plan and is chalked on stage floor when setting up.
CLEAT	Attachment on back of flat for securing a throwline; also affixed to fly rail for tying off hemp lines.
CLOTH *DROP*	As BACKCLOTH.
COUNTERWEIGHT SYSTEM	A mechanical method of moving barrels or pipes from stage level to grid level; and compensating for weight of scenery tied to barrel by adding or subtracting weights.

CRADLE	A housing for weights used in the above COUNTER-WEIGHT SYSTEM.
CUT CLOTH *CUT-OUT DROP*	Similar scene-canvas as backcloth, but has been cut out in the centre in leaf shapes, etc.
CUT-OUT or PROFILE FLAT	A flat with ply-wood edge cut in silhouette.
CYCLORAMA	A curved backcloth hanging in approximately a semi-circle at the rear of the stage, and sometimes extending at either side to the proscenium arch. It is usually painted in one colour to give the effect of sky or infinity. Sometimes built as a permanent fixture in plaster or other material.
DIMMER	A general term for various appliances such as rheostats, transformers and thyristors by which the intensity of light can be varied.
DIP *FLOOR-POCKET*	A small metal trap in the stage floor covering dimmer outlet sockets, into which leads for lighting equipment used on the stage floor can be plugged.
DOWNSTAGE	Nearest the audience.
EXTENDING BRACE, *EXTENSION BRACE*	See BRACE.
FALSE PROSCENIUM, *PORTAL OPENING*	Temporary proscenium set within the permanent opening.
FESTOON	A curtain with several lines passing through rings which are sewn to webbing on the reverse side. By this means the curtain can be draped in swags.
FLAT	A rectangular wooden frame covered with scene-canvas.
FLOOD or SCOOP	Lamp with a diffusing reflector giving a wide spread of light – suspended above stage or fixed on a stand in the wings.
FLY FLOOR *FLY GALLERY*	Narrow platform or gallery above stage (usually on both side walls) from which flymen raise or lower scenery and lighting equipment by pulling on the lines. Sometimes a fly bridge across back wall connects side fly floors.
FLY RAIL *PIN RAIL*	A railing on stage side of FLY FLOOR to which hemp lines are made off on a CLEAT.
FOOTLIGHTS or FLOATS	A trough divided into compartments (as in a batten) situated in the foremost part of the stage at floor level.
FORESTAGE	Another word for APRON.
FRENCH BRACE *JACK*	Wooden support hinged to a FLAT.
FRENCH FLAT	Two or three flats battened together for flying.
FRONT OF HOUSE (F.O.H.) LIGHTING *AUDITORIUM BEAM*	Spotlights in the auditorium focused on the front of the stage.
FROST	A gelatin resembling frosted or ground glass for diffusing light.
GAUZE	A fine-woven mesh that can be painted to look solid when lit from the front and backed with a black curtain; transparent when lit from behind and the black backing removed.
GELATIN	A colour medium or filter for lighting.

GET IN *TAKE IN*	The bringing of scenery, costumes, etc., into a theatre.
GET OUT *TAKE OUT*	The reverse of above.
GRID *GRIDIRON*	Steel or wood framework, immediately below the stage ceiling, from which scenery and lighting equipment is suspended by either counterweight or hemp line system.
GROUND ROW (Scenic)	A narrow rectangular flat on its side — often with a profiled edge. Functionally it conceals lighting of backcloth or cyclorama.
GROUND ROW (Lighting)	A trough (similar to Footlights) lighting bottom section of backcloth or cyclorama.
GRUMMET	Loop of rope or wire line used either as a guide or tie-off point.
HANGING IRON	Iron plate with ring, screwed to flat as a fixing point for rope or wire lines used for flying the flat.
HEMP LINES	Man-handled lines as opposed to COUNTERWEIGHT SYSTEM.
HOUSE CURTAIN OR HOUSE TABS	The permanent front curtain.
LEG *LEG DROP*	Narrow pieces of painted canvas or curtains hung vertically as side masking from border height to stage level.
LIFT *ELEVATOR*	Mechanical method of creating various stage levels by raising or lowering sections of the stage.
LINE	Any rope or hemp line (hanging from the grid) that is guiding or holding hung scenery.
LOADING FLOOR *LOADING BRIDGE*	Gallery above fly floor from which counterweight cradles are loaded.
MASK	To hide or screen off parts of the stage from the view of the audience.
OPPOSITE PROMPT (O.P.) *STAGE RIGHT*	The right-hand side of stage when facing auditorium.
PACK *STACK*	Scenery in wings or dock ready for use.
PAGEANT *PARABOLIC REFLECTOR FLOOD*	Strong directional light, slightly diffused. Now often replaced by soft edge spot.
PAINT FRAME	Large wooden frame on to which a cloth or run of flats is nailed for painting from a bridge. The frame or bridge can be raised or lowered.
PERCH *TORMENTOR SPOT*	Downstage spotlight behind the side of the proscenium, usually above head height. (Platform on which spotlight is mounted is also known as PERCH).
PLATE *KEYSTONE*	Plywood piece for re-inforcing a joint on any kind of frame; particularly used with a butt joint.
PRIMING	Preparatory coat of thin size or size and colour on new canvas; also for obliterating coat on old canvas to be re-painted.
PROFILE SPOT	Hard edge spotlight.
PROJECTOR	Spotlight designed to throw a painted or photographic image (or moving effects such as clouds, etc.) by means of a slide on to a backcloth.
PROMPT SIDE (P.S.) *STAGE LEFT*	The left-hand side of the stage when facing auditorium.

PROPERTIES (PROPS)	Objects such as furniture, etc., used in the action of the play and too small to be classified as scenery.
PROSCENIUM	The stage opening that separates the auditorium from the stage.
RAIL	Horizontal member of flat frame.
RAKE	Floor which slopes from back down to front of stage.
RETURN	Flat leading 'off' at right angle to another.
REVEAL *THICKNESS*	Surround of arch, window, door, etc., at right angle to face of flat.
ROSTRUM *PARALLEL*	Temporary platform for raising a part of the stage.
SANDWICH BATTEN	Double battening for cloths.
SETTING LINE	Line parallel with footlights, and upstage of house curtain, from which setting of scenery is measured. It should be shown on designer's ground plan.
SILL *SADDLE IRON*	Flat iron bar spanning the foot of a door opening or archway for strength.
SIZE *SIZING*	Thin glue in powder or gelatine form which acts as a fixative to scene paint.
SPOT BAR *LIGHT PIPE*	Counterweighted barrel from which lighting equipment is hung above stage.
SPOT LINE	Single line dropped from the grid to an exact mark on the stage.
STAGE CLOTH *GROUND CLOTH* or *FLOORCLOTH*	Specially woven cloth stretched tightly across stage floor.
STAGE DIRECTOR *PRODUCTION STAGE MANAGER*	The senior technician responsible for all technical activities on stage.
STAGE SCREW	Screw for securing stage brace to floor.
STAGE WEIGHTS	Iron weight for holding stage brace in position.
STILE	Vertical member of flat frame.
TABS	Usually refers to house curtain but also general term applied to any curtains used on stage.
THROWLINE *LASHLINE*	Line temporarily securing two flats together by means of cleats and a slip knot.
TOGGLE *KEYSTONE*	Means of attaching centre rail(s) of a frame of a flat to the stiles. These rails are thus known as toggle rails.
TORMENTOR	Masking flat (usually black) immediately behind the proscenium and running upstage as far as the setting line and/or false proscenium.
TRANSPARENCY	A thin unprimed cloth painted thinly in dye colours and lit from behind.
TRAP	Trap-door cut anywhere in stage floor between joists.
TRAVERSE CURTAIN *TRAVELLER*	Curtains hung on a track which can be opened or closed across stage.
TRUCK WAGGON	Rostrum on wheels, carrying a setting or part of a setting.
WINGS	Sides of stage masked from audience's view by wing flats (or legs) which are set parallel to setting line or angled upstage.

BIBLIOGRAPHY

SCENIC DESIGN, GENERAL, Etc.

On the Art of the Theatre by Edward Gordon Craig : William Heinemann, London 1911

Settings and Costumes of the Modern Stage by Theodore Komisarjevsky and Lee Simonson : The Studio Ltd, London 1933

Film and Theatre by Allardyce Nicoll : George G. Harrap and Co. Ltd, U.S.A. 1936

New Theatres for Old by Mordecai Gorelik : Dobson Books Ltd, London 1940

Ballet Design : Past and Present by Cyril W. Beaumont : The Studio Ltd, London 1940

Art in Modern Ballet by George Amberg : Pantheon Books Inc, New York 1947

The Art of Scenic Design by Lee Simonson : Harper and Brothers Publishers, New York 1950

Drama : Its Costume and Décor by James Laver : The Studio Ltd, London 1951

Theatre-in-the-Round by Margo Jones : Rinehart and Co. Inc, New York 1951

The Open Stage by Richard Southern : Faber and Faber Ltd, London 1953

Stage Design Throughout the World Since 1935, Edited by R. Hainaux : George Harrap and Co. Ltd, London 1956

Stage Scenery and Lighting by Samuel Selden and Hunton D. Sellman : Appleton-Century-Crosts Inc, New York 1959

Television by Design by Richard Levin : The Bodley Head, London 1961

The Stage is Set by Lee Simonson : Theatre Arts Books, New York 1963

Scene Design and Stage Lighting by W. Oren Parker and Harvey K. Smith : Holt, Rinehart and Winston Inc, New York 1963

Stage Design Throughout the World Since 1950, Edited by R. Hainaux : George Harrap and Co. Ltd, London 1964

Scene Painting and Design by Stephen Joseph : Sir Isaac Pitman and Sons Ltd, London 1964

Designing for the Theatre by Jo Mielziner : New York Atheneum, 1965

Designing and Making Stage Scenery by Michael Warre : Studio Vista, London 1966 ; Reinhold, New York

LIGHTING

Theatrical Lighting Practice by Joel E. Rubin and Leland H. Watson : Theatre Arts Books, New York 1954

Stage Lighting by Theodore Fuchs : Benjamin Blom, Inc, New York 1963

COSTUME

Modes and Manners by Max von Boehm, Trans. by Joan Joshua : 9 Vols. George G. Harrap and Co. Ltd, London 1932–1935

The Book of Costume by Millia Davenport : Crown Publishers, New York 1949

Designing and Making Stage Costumes by Motley : Studio Vista, London 1964 ; Watson Guptill, New York

History of Costume by Blanche Payne : Harper and Row, Publishers, New York 1965

Costume in Pictures by Phillis Cunnington : Studio Vista, London 1964 ; E. P. Dutton, New York